Cryptocurrency

Everything you need to know about Bitcoin,
Ethereum,Blockchain, Before Investing In It

Contents

Introduction

Ever wondered what contributed to the Bitcoin boom? It has taken away the global market by a boom. Within a short span of time, it has crossed some major milestones, and you might be wondering, how it all started.

Apart from the fact that Bitcoins are decentralized, the fact that it was the first cryptocurrency to work on blockchain technology, contributed to its success. Blockchain technology is something that most major systems in the world will have to depend on in the near future, and we will take a look at it in detail below.

In this eBook, we will take a look at the major cryptocurrency bitcoin, how popular alternatives like Etherium are the way to go if you are looking to make money through cryptocurrency, how blockchain technology works, and how you could make the best investments. We will take a look at all that you need to know about cryptocurrencies itself, and how they can differ from each other.

Chapter 1

Origin of Bitcoin

Its basic origin dates back to early 2008, when the whole world suffered an economic collapse. A breakdown was on the way for the global market. It was during this time that the various economic reforms were to be performed to get the market out of a chaotic situation. A central monetary agency was held responsible for checking the reforming measures that could be taken in every possible way to find a solution.

During this situation of crisis, the first idea of blockchain was conceptualized in early 2008, by an anonymous person or group, known as Satoshi Nakamoto. Nobody really knows who he is - though he is theorized to be a Japanese - but in 2009, Bitcoin started to serve as the public ledger for all transactions. The invention of the blockchain model for Bitcoin made it the first digital currency available in the world to solve the double spending problem without any need of a costlier trusted authority or expensive central server. The blockchain is the main innovation of Bitcoin.

During this situation, a revolutionary idea of Virtual transactions or Cashless currency was put forward by a fictitious person or group named Satoshi Nakamoto. This idea had both pros and cons. The pros were that it was completely decentralized.

A method that was most sought after by the common people. They would directly connect with their peers for any transaction related activities. But the demerit was that it had a market-based centralization. But looking for the most important advantage - the decentralization, Bitcoin became the most popular and most powerful crypto currency.

Crypto Currency- What Is It?

To elaborate on Cryptocurrency, it is a type of digital currency, in which the issuing and accounting of transactions are based on crypto graphic methods. It involves the Proof of work protection method and has asymmetric encryption, and thus the system functions in manner that is decentralized in a distributed computer network system.

Also, in the case of crypto currency, it is not at all possible to cancel or return the funds sent to the payee. However, there are several opportunities for continuing transactions involving any intermediary in between, when the required consent of all three or any two parties is must to complete or even cancel the transaction. And the balance cannot be frozen forcibly or recovered without access to the owner's private password key phrase, although the parties of the transaction do have the option to temporarily block their funds as collateral, voluntarily.

Presently, all the currently existing crypto currencies are used anonymously - all transactions are available to public, but there is no particular default binding to a particular person, although the customer's identity can be easily established if the necessary additional private information can be found.

Understanding Bitcoins

Now, let's have some more insights into the usage of this revolutionary idea of Bitcoin. To start with, one should have installed a Bitcoin wallet application on his computer or mobile phone, which will pave the way to generate a first Bitcoin address and more addresses can be created whenever there arises any necessity. Once the address is generated, it should be disclosed to the peers, relatives or friends so that they can pay or vice versa. This is almost similar to how an electronic mail works, except the fact that the Bitcoin addresses generated can be used only once.

The blockchain technology is nothing but a shared public ledger on which the entire system of the Bitcoin network depends. All the successful transactions are put forward in the block chain. In this way, Bitcoin wallets do calculate their user's balance amount that is spendable and new transactions can be verified to be a set of spending Bitcoins that are basically owned by the user of the wallet. The integrity, security and the order of transactions of the blockchain are confirmed with the method of advanced cryptography.

How Does Bitcoin Transfers Take Place?

In the blockchain method, you transfer values between Bitcoin wallets that are added to the network of the blockchain. All users have a called a private key or seed, and each time you login to your Bitcoin wallet, it is this code that you need to enter offering a method that prevents transaction from being tampered with by any other person. All the blockchain transactions are broadcast between its users and relayed for as many as ten minutes to avoid any tampering.

What is Mining?

Users can create Bitcoin using a process called mining. Mining acts as a record-keeping service which utilizes the processing power of the computer.

Miners are responsible for keeping the Bitcoin blockchain consistent, unalterable and complete. Their job is to verify and collect the newly broadcasted transactions into blocks over and over again. All the blocks are designed to have a cryptographic hash of block that comes before it and that acts as a link creating an unending chain.

All new blocks have to become eligible to join this chain first. They must have a proof-of-work which means that the miners are required to find a number which is commonly referred to as the nonce. If the block content is hashed with this number, the result would be lesser than the Bitcoin network's difficulty target. While nodes can verify this proof result, it is difficult to create this cryptographic hash. It also takes time because miners use a hit and trial method.

The difficulty target depends upon the recent performance of the network and is altered after every 2,016 blocks. The objective is to maintain an average time of ten minutes between new blocks. As a result, the system adjusts itself to the mining power available.

The proof-of-work system, when combined with the chaining of blocks, is a strong security protections against attackers who want to modify the blockchain in some manner. A hacker has to keep changing the subsequent blocks if he wants the system to accept even one modified block.

There are new blocks being formed and mined all the time which only increases the amount of difficulty one might face when tampering with the blockchain. The blocks are cut off from the system when the Bitcoin transactions are finalized.

Miners also have the option of creating Bitcoin with the help of a special software that is useful in solving cryptographic problems. Not only will one be able to issue Bitcoin easily, but also be encouraged to mine more. However, the system lays down a fixed number of Bitcoin that can be in circulation at a specific point in time.

The process of mining is a distributed evaluation method that is used to confirm all the transactions in the queue by adding them in the blockchain. It is also held responsible for maintaining a chronological order in the processing of blockchain, helps in protecting the neutrality of the blockchain network, and allows various user computers to agree on the present state of the network system. For the transactions to be confirmed, all the transactions must be firmly packed in a data block that suits all the strict cryptographic protocol rules that will be, at a later instant of time, verified by the network system.

The process of mining is intentionally designed to be resource intensive in nature and also be difficult so that the always the number of blocks found each day by the miners remains steady in nature. Each block must always contain a proof about the work that is to be considered as valid. This proof of work is verified by other existing Bitcoin nodes each and every time they receive a fresh block. Bitcoin uses the method of hash cash proof of work functioning.

Bitcoins, so issued with the help of mining process are the best way to hold the anonymity of transaction during the work, with crypto currency. Or else, they can be put into use only after getting hundreds of network confirmations.

The term Bitcoin mining is so called because it almost resembles the procedure of mining of other materials. That is, it needs the process of exertion, and it gradually makes new currency available slowly at a rate that resembles the rate at which materials like gold and silver are excavated and mined from the crust of the earth.

The interesting fact about Bitcoin mixers are the services used by the clients to create a misdirection of the originality of actual clients' Bitcoins. In simpler terms, it cleans the dirty money circulating in the system. Although the services provided aren't free, they charge a small fee. Nowadays the Bitcoin mixers across the world trade a particular clients' Bitcoins with other people's at random offer either for better or for their worse. But the fact is. Unfortunately, this also includes trading a client's Bitcoins with other people's tainted Bitcoins that could be related to any drug money or any other ones funded as black money that is now connected to innocent client's wallet.

These protocol rules prevent any existing previous blocks from being tampered or modified at a later instant because happening of such things would make all the next following blocks of data to fail or make them invalid. The process of mining also makes a secure system of a data network that prevents any individual user from quickly and easily adding new data blocks consecutively in the system of the block chain. In this way, no individuals, or no system can have a control on what is included in the block chain or attempt to replace the parts of the block chain network to send back their own spending up details.

Why should one prefer investing in Bitcoin?

After getting to know the way in which this block chain system works, the next question that arises in mind is why should one invest in this Bitcoin. And the various reasons can be provided to support the investment in Bitcoin.

Some of the reasons to invest in Bitcoin!

- The system of Bitcoin is completely decentralized one, and it has always been free from centralized bank manipulation schemes and government policies.

- Nowadays more and more people, businesses have already started using Bitcoin.

- And a fact is well known that just like gold and silver, Bitcoin's value does not at all correlate with the existing fiat currency and always tends to move in the way opposite to existing stocks and bonds available in the market as of present day.

- Also, in comparison to gold or silver, Bitcoin has been mostly undervalued at the present moment.

- The important and notable fact is that the supply of Bitcoins is limited. As of a now, only around twenty million Bitcoins have ever be mined, once the last edition of Bitcoin is mined, the value of bitcoin will rise abruptly which may happen, by the looks of it, may happen in just a few years or the very nearby future.

- Bitcoins are decentralized by all the ways, and one will have to worry only about the true market.

 Forces existing at that instant of time.

- Nowadays people do prefer Blockchains in order to revolutionize the storage methods and also the transaction methods in the coming future.

- As a matter of fact, using a Blockchain ensures the user a higher speed as well as security at a lower cost and ensures a lesser margin for errors that may take place during the usual transaction.

- The decentralized system of blockchain database always keeps its records open to the public so that everything is easily verifiable and also ensures that all the transactions remain transparent.

- Also, a hacker will find it extremely difficult to attack a secure network that is always being hosted by millions of computers connected to a network at the same time.

To summarize, the Bitcoin model is expanding slowly towards the target but also steadily. Along with that, the technical community is also working hard to find any other available ways on how the block chain technology can be used in other fields and sectors other than finance.

The Financial Benefits as an Investor

The technology behind the Bitcoin is pseudonymous, which means that the funds are not linked or related to any of the real world physical entities but rather are nothing but Bitcoin addresses. The users or owners of Bitcoin address are not directly identified, but all their transactions done on the blockchain are made public.

1. Link all transactions

In addition to this, all the transactions can be linked to the individuals and the enlisted companies in terms of usage. For example, all the transactions that tend to spend Bitcoins from multiple input channels do indicate that the inputs may have originated from a common user and confirmatory public transactional data with any known information about users of particular addresses.

2. Use Bitcoin Exchanges

Additionally, Bitcoin exchanges do exist, wherein Bitcoins are traded for the traditional currencies, but here the law may ask to collect the data regarding to personal information of the user.

3. Generate A Bitcoin Address

To strengthen the financial privacy of a particular user, a new Bitcoin address can be regenerated for every transaction. Let us consider an example, these block chain wallets generate some anonymous random rolling addresses for each and every transaction from a particular single seed created by a user, while the only requirement being a single password phrase key to be remembered by the user to recover all the corresponding private password phrase keys. Researchers have also shown evidence that Bitcoin exchanges and other related entities can provide required supporting proof for assets, liabilities, solvency without revealing the originating addresses using zero-knowledge proofs of user data.

4. Know Your Rules

On account of Bitcoin's decentralized system nature, nations or states cannot shut down the system network or try to alter its protocol related technical rules. However, the use of

Bitcoin can be treated to be a criminal offense, and the attempt of shutting down exchanges and the peer to peer economy in a given country can be constituted in its law to ban this crypto currency system.

The actual legal status of Bitcoin system varies substantially from country to country and is still found to be undefined or changing in many of the countries across the world. While in some countries, the law has explicitly allowed its usage and trade, many others have either banned or restricted it. Rules, regulations, and bans that apply to Bitcoin probably extend in a similar way as to other existing cryptocurrency systems present in the world.

5. Do You Intend to Mine?

Regarding the power consumption, the Bitcoin has always been criticized for the huge amounts of electricity being consumed by mining. In order to lower the cost of usage, Bitcoin miners have set up inventories in places like Iceland wherein the Geo thermal energy is cheap and the cooling Arctic air is probably free. As far as the time is concerned, the Chinese Bitcoin miners are found to use hydroelectric power in order to reduce the electricity costs.

The Peer to Peer Network

Presently the Bitcoin transactions and its following emission are regulated by an extensive peer to peer network. This Bitcoin technology uses a distributed public as well as a universal database that is spread through a decentralized channel of peer to peer networking that uses the digital signatures and happens to be supported by a proof of work protocol that ensures a customer with security and legitimacy of funds that have been put in use

To guarantee that a third party user, who cannot spend other people's Bitcoins creates transactions in their names, using a public key cryptography method. This way, it is also easy to verify the digital signatures of the party.

Getting Your Own Keys

Every investor has their own public and private keys which they need to hold in a secured wallet. Only when you give the private keys can you access your account, and only when you give your public keys can you make a transfer.

Today Bitcoin has emerged to be the most widely spread cryptocurrency system. Its current total market value estimates to be over a Hundred billion dollar. A user can exchange, buy or sell Bitcoins on many online sites. Despite the fact that usage of Bitcoin does not formally require any user identification, the currency has not remained completely anonymous.

Can Bitcoin Mining Work Now?

Formerly, to speed up the initial stages system, Bitcoin mining was designed in a way to bribe away the early users or customers with exponentially better gains than the latecomers could get for the similar effort. In its present state and as predicted for the near future, as a part of its basic design curve, it is not at all feasible for a newcomer in the Bitcoin to mine his own assets in this segment. The present economies of scale are also far too large to be handled, and home PC equipment has been obsolete with regards to the latest trend in the technological space.

So, in order to join the network today, new users must instead put in the ever-rising amount of wealth to previously holding Bitcoiners who are sitting around in the space, doing nothing. This collectively makes Bitcoin a haven for early entrants, who have more Bitcoins than anyone else in the segment ever, accumulated no risk. Some believe they hyped it up so that they can offload their existing Bitcoins - however, it's just a hypothesis that has never been tested. For now, it does seem a good investment and the amount is only expected to go up in the near future.

At the same instant of time those speculators, who are providing all of their available capital or the amount of money Bitcoin is actually worth is delimited to the amount of the fiat currency placed out in the Bitcoin exchanges as it is found that is the only way new value shall enter the present ecosystem and taking away all of the risks of assumed crash, are chasing far lower amount of percentage returns than the initial users would receive.

The Final Verdict

This also means that the system runs on opportunism, especially among those people who like the idea of decentralized technology as well as money. This setup is always defended as an acceptable area of trade-off and a fair, rewarding method for propping up the current system.

According to one study, only twenty-two percent of existing Bitcoins were in circulation at all. There were a total of seventy plus active users and businesses. Interestingly, the finding also stated that one unidentified customer owned a quarter of all Bitcoins in existing circulation.

And one large owner was trying to hide all their available wealth accumulation by moving it in and around in thousands of smaller chunks of transactions. Meanwhile, businesses, ranging from family stores to the multi-million dollar corporates, have jumped onto the stream of Bitcoin already to seem forward-looking and get a cut of the Bitcoin trade.

When a Bitcoin transaction takes place, it's just a change in the system of Blockchain itself. But what I suggest is go on, dive in and get rich.

Chapter 2 -

Do you need a Bitcoin wallet?

Wallets are an easy way to store essential information virtually. Having a wallet will help you make Bitcoin transactions with more relative ease.

A common myth is that the wallets are meant to hold the Bitcoins. However, the system makes it impossible to separate the Bitcoins from the extensive blockchain transaction ledger. This wallet records all your digital credentials that are required for your Bitcoin holdings. As a result, you can access them whenever you like and use them as payment.

The Bitcoin network is based on public-key cryptography. This means that it generates one public and one private cryptographic key. The wallet collects these keys and stores the data for future use.

Bitcoin offers you several options when it comes to choosing a wallet that is perfect for your needs. These software wallets remain connected to the network which means that you can use them for transactions as well. You can choose among:

Full clients:

Once you have a full client wallet, you will be able to verify transactions on a local copy or a subset of the blockchain directly. Secure and unreliable, it will not require you to trust external parties who have not earned it. Full clients are responsible for checking the validity of mined blocks. This eliminates the chance of transactions occurring in a chain which breaks or changes the network rules. The size and complexity of the network prevent it from being suitable for all computing devices. This wallet acts like a standalone email server which does not depend on any third-party servers to get the work done.

Lightweight clients:

If you opt to be a lightweight client, you can consult a full client in case you want to send and receive transactions. You will not even need a local copy of the blockchain. It is much easier and less time-consuming to set up lightweight clients. Moreover, you can run them on low-power and conserve energy. If you prefer using your smartphone over your computer, then being a lightweight client will be ideal for you because the network will run properly even on low-bandwidth devices. The only drawback of having this wallet is that user must place a certain degree of faith on the server. Since lightweight clients do not have to check the validity of the blockchain, they have to trust the miners to do it for them. The user has to keep the private keys safe to guard it against misuse.

Web client:

Being a web client means that you are subscribing to services that are nothing like that of the full client wallet. This wallet is completely dependent on a third-party server which then carries out the entire transaction. All the credentials that are required to access funds in the Bitcoin account are entrusted with the online wallet provider. Users have to develop a relationship based on trust if they want this method of Bitcoin transaction to be successful.

If you are new to Bitcoin, you can choose any of these three wallets to start the process.

Downsides:

Bitcoin is not completely free of the chance for people to run scams. The common Ponzi scams are basically high-yield investment programs which tempt you with a higher interest rate than the existing market rate. Then the money is transferred into an account that belongs to the group of scammers. They can hide their identity well, so beware.

There are also Bitcoin mining scams which constitute companies offering to pay you an enormous amount of Bitcoin if you pay them a certain value. You can be sure that you will never get hold of the company or the promised Bitcoins after that.

On the other hand, Bitcoin Exchange Scams will give you access to brilliant features that your normal wallet does not. Do not fall into that trap.

Bitcoin wallet scams have been doing the rounds for quite a while now where you are directly asked for your money. The address provided will transfer the funds to them instead of you.

Conclusion:

All said and done, Bitcoin with its transparency and security is heralding the future of both finance and computation. It is well worth your investment.

Chapter 3

Moving on to Blockchain

What Do You Need to Know About Blockchain?

Blockchain is what is the future of financial transactions, and the future of keeping data. It helps track processes minutely, and enabled a secure proof way of transferring them over one network to another at minimal cost. We would take a look at how it works below.

History:

The idea of a chain that would be secured by cryptography first found its way to the world through the minds of Stuart Haber and W. Scott Stornetta. Bayer, Haber and Stornetta introduced Merkle trees to their design of a blockchain which enhanced the design further. Th blockchain would now allow a large number of documents to be collected into it.

As mentioned before, the blockchain database is operated by a timestamping server automatically. Nakamoto introduced the blockchain in 2008 and then waited a year to use it for the digital currency bitcoin. The blockchain is the only reason Bitcoin was able to eliminate the double spending problem and that has been a major contributor to its popularity.

It was in 2014 that the bitcoin blockchain made a record when the storage size reached 20 GB. It contained the records every transaction that had ever been done through the blockchain. By 2015, the figure almost reached 30GB, after which there was a phenomenal rise. Between January 2016 and January 2017, the size of the Bitcoin blockchain became 100 GB from just 50GB to 100GB.

Satoshi Nakamoto had intended the term to be, 'block chain' but the single word blockchain had gained more momentum by 2016.

The introduction of blockchain 2.0 further revolutionised the concept of a blockchain. It incorporated several new applications to the distributed blockchain database. This second-generation programmable blockchain was a boon for all industries alike. Blockchain 2.0 technology could be used to perform important functions other than just transactions. You could exchange almost anything of value as long as you were a part of this global economy.

The second-generation blockchain technology has been programmed in such a manner that it can store an individual's digital ID and persona. Some say that it has the potential to help eradicate the wealth gap which still exists in the world.

Blockchain and Advanced Security:

As mentioned before, a blockchain is decentralized and hence eliminates the risk of hackers getting access to the one storage space that contains all data. The network does not have any centralized point of vulnerability that makes it susceptible to the attack of computer hackers. The "username/password" system which most of us to keep our identity private and protect our data and assets online can be easily bypassed which means that there is a high security risk involved.

On the other hand, blockchain technology uses dual keys and an encryption method that is difficult to beat. These public and private "keys" help a person keep their identity a secret because they cannot be traced back to a particular individual.

A "public key" refers to a rather long but randomly-generated string composed of numbers. This is the user address one has on the blockchain and any transaction to or from it will only be able to give out just the public key. Even the most advanced hackers will not be able to connect it to the private key.

Coming to private keys, they are a password which helps the owner access their digital assets which are stored on the blockchain network. Nobody but you should know about this particular string of numbers. As long as you keep it a secret, your data will practically be almost incorruptible.

Bitcoin and Blockchain Technology :

There is a common myth that Bitcoin and blockchain are one and the same. The myth arises from the fact that both were devised just a year apart from each other, but it is not true. Bitcoin is a simple cryptocurrency that depends on the system of blockchain to work efficiently. Here, one has to know why Satoshi developed the blockchain in order to introduce Bitcoin to the world.

A blockchain is extremely convenient since it requires minimum maintenance. Since there is no trusted central authority, the users do not have to place their faith where they do not want to.

There is a network of communicating nodes which are responsible for keeping the software going. The network nodes have the power to validate all your transactions and make the record in the global ledger so that it can be broadcasted to other nodes.

Since the blockchain is a distributed database, all the network nodes have to store a copy of it so that independent verification can be performed. A fresh group of transactions also called a block, is created and becomes a part of the blockchain almost six times in every hour. The information is also published on the nodes.

The blockchain can help one to find out how much currency has been used to eliminate chances of double-spending. Unlike a conventional ledger which keeps a track of bills or promissory notes, a blockchain represents Bitcoin transactions as unspent outputs.

Miners verify and collect the newly broadcasted transactions into blocks over and over again. All the blocks are designed to have a cryptographic hash of block that comes before it and that acts as a link creating an unending chain.

All new blocks have to become eligible to join this chain first. They must have a proof-of-work which means that the miners are required to find a number which is commonly referred to as the nonce. If the block content is hashed with this number, the result would be lesser than the Bitcoin network's difficulty target. While nodes can verify this proof result, it is difficult to create this cryptographic hash. It also takes time because miners use a hit and trial method.

The difficulty target depends upon the recent performance of the network and is altered after every 2,016 blocks. The objective is to maintain an average time of ten minutes between new blocks. As a result, the system adjusts itself to the mining power available.

The proof-of-work system, when combined with the chaining of blocks, is a strong security protections against attackers who want to modify the blockchain in some manner. A hacker has to keep changing the subsequent blocks if he wants the system to accept even one modified block.

There are new blocks being formed and mined all the time which only increases the amount of difficulty one might face when tampering with the blockchain. The blocks are cut off from the system when the transactions are finalized.

Features of Blockchain:

A blockchain has a set of unique features which makes it special among the various digital innovations of the 21st century.

The transactions you make are irreversible:

Once you make a transaction with the help of a blockchain and receive a confirmation that it has been successful, you will not be able to reverse it under any circumstance. In fact, none of the network members will be able to help you out either. There is no loophole that you can take advantage of to undo the transaction altogether. Once you send money, you cannot get it back. Even if there is a mistake that needs to be straightened, the system is such that it allows no room for reversing transactions. Since there is no safety net, it is best that you always think things through before transferring funds in a blockchain.

Be Absolutely Secure:

As we have mentioned before, the main advantage of transacting or doing almost anything with blockchain is that the security system in place is almost impenetrable. The world's best cryptographers have worked on developing the blockchain system which is reassuring to all users. Since the network is public and can be easily verified, hackers will find it difficult to mess with.

Your wishes are the only ones that matter:

When it comes to using cryptocurrency using a blockchain, you are free to begin and stop anytime you want. There is no hard and fast rule that binds you to the system or prevents you from joining it in the first place. You do not need to get permission from a particular group of people or a body. You can download the free software and get going without any hassle. A blockchain does not have a gatekeeper because it is totally decentralized.

It is spread across the world but still maintains a high speed when doing the work:

If you want a system that is not only fast and efficient but also has a global reach, then blockchain fits the bill perfectly. Any transaction that you begin will be propagated within just a few seconds across the network in the network no matter how far you are from the real-life location of the addressee. You will receive a confirmation of the success of your transaction very soon. The global network of computers does not take your physical location into account which is what makes blockchain a growing global entity in the world of finance.

What can Blockchain be used for?

What started out as a tool for improving the virtual world of finance, is now equipped to be useful for almost every other business. You do not have to know extensively about Blockchain in order to use it.

Bitcoin has become a global cryptocurrency because of its blockchain network, as a result of which the technology still finds maximum usage in the world of finance. Anybody who devises a new digital currency needs to develop a blockchain in order to make it successful. Since it helps cut out the middleman in every type of transactions, the general public is appreciative of these wallets that keep their financial record flawlessly.

Now, blockchains are used by different companies to collect data on their sales and compile them. The permanent and transparent ledger system helps a business to progress by minimising human contribution. The digital entity takes over and it can be programmed in a manner such that all tasks can be performed with the least amount of labour.

A blockchain is also used as a tracking service for keeping an eye on value parts which have found its way to the supply chain.

Even major counties are going out of their way to incorporate blockchains in the digital sector. For example, Russia has been successful in making the very first government-level blockchain implementation. Also, the bank Sberbank partnered with Russia's Federal Antimonopoly Service (FAS) in 2017 because they want to work on the concept of document transfer and storage using blockchains.

Online transactions that happen through a blockchain are linked to an elaborate process of identity verification. Blockchain wallet apps might become a way of identity management in the coming years.

What does Blockchain offer?

You might be wondering how businesses will benefit from using Blockchain.

Smart contracts:

Since blockchains are distributed ledgers, they can help you code simple contracts which will be automatically executed when a set of conditions are met. Smart contracts are flexible and you can program them to perform even the simplest functions with relative ease. These contracts are beneficial to a growing business.

Governance:

A blockchain gives you access to a network that is not only completely transparent but also can be accessed publicly. The concept of a distributed database can help make elections corruption-free. Any poll which has a chance of falling prey to illegal activities can be automated with the help of blockchain.

Crowdfunding:

For quite a while now, crowdfunding has become a popular way to raise money for attractive project ventures. The public wants to contribute directly to product development. Blockchains help raise crowd-sourced venture capital funds because it makes the system of payment so easy. A lot of platforms are utilizing it now.

Sharing economy:

The concept of a sharing economy has gained momentum in the last few years. A blockchain enables peer-to-peer payments which means that parties can directly interact with each other and that is the foundation for a decentralized sharing economy.

Supply chain auditing:

Customers are becoming more aware by the day and want to know the elaborate details of any product they invest in. They want to make sure that the ethical claims made by a company are founded on truth. Distributed ledgers can help one track the history anything that we buy. We can verify if a product is genuine because of the blockchain time-stamping method.

File storage:

Have you ever felt the panic of accidentally deleting a folder which had all your important files? It can also happen in the virtual world. An easy solution to this problem is decentralizing your file storage system. Since the data is distributed across the network, the risk of hacking or losing is reduced.

Protection of intellectual property:

The downside of the Internet is that anybody can copy digital information and pass it off as their own. While this distribution of data is what makes the Internet so important for us, copyright holders often suffer by losing out on their intellectual property. With the help of smart contracts, once can automate distribution and sale of creative works.

Prediction markets:

You can crowdsource predictions based simply on event probability using the blockchain network. They turn out to be highly accurate because the average opinion if free of undue biases. There are a large number of prediction markets which reward people on correct guesses using blockchains.

Identity management:

The web needs a superior system of identity management because virtual commerce hinges on it. Any transaction that happens needs to be properly verified. Blockchains, being distributed ledgers, will help you organize your digital identity and allow you to prove it.

Stock trading:

Blockchains make share settlement much easier in the world of stock trading. Th peer-to-peer transactions help make trade confirmations instantaneous by removing all the intermediaries. A large number of stock and commodities exchanges are already prototyping applications based on blockchain for this purpose.

Conclusion:

Blockchains are a revolutionary piece of technology which will change the Internet as we know it. Being a part of this change and adapting to it is important.

Chapter 4 –

All You Need To Know About Ethereum

Introduction:

If you are into technology, you might have heard about the public platform, Ethereum. The working of this open-source computing platform which runs on the principle of the blockchain is embedded in advanced software developments. Ethereum was born when Vitalik Buterin, a cryptocurrency programmer, proposed the idea in 2013. The funding for the project came from an online crowd sale which was held in 2014. Developed by a Swiss nonprofit organization called the Ethereum Foundation, the platform soon became very popular among tech enthusiasts.

In case you are planning to invest in this platform, it is best that you know all about its various aspects. However, to understand how Ethereum functions and why it is taking the digital by storm, you have to learn about blockchain first.

The DAO Project:

The DAO project collapsed in 2016 causing Ethereum to break down into two different blockchains - Ethereum (ETH), and Ethereum Classic (ETC). However, the story runs deeper.

Ethereum, because of its decentralized nature, is known to be hack-proof. However, 2016 was witness to an event that changed the course of the platform forever. A startup which was creating a DOA project called 'The DAO' was hacked and that led to a large number of problems.

Developed and programmed by a team from Slock.it which was another startup, the project wanted to establish a humanless venture capital firm. Investors would be able to take sensible decisions through smart contracts. The project was funded through a token sale and was extremely profitable in the long run.

However, as soon as the project earned enough funds to get going, an unknown attacker hacked it and stole a significant portion of Ether that would amount to $50 million dollars. After much research, it was found that a technical glitch in The DAO software has been the cause of the hack. Still, Ethereum was left to gather up the broken pieces and make the best of the situation.

The Ethereum community took a decision to retrieve the stolen Ether with the help of a hard fork. In layman's terms, they wanted to change the code itself. The stolen funds were transferred to a new smart contract that was programmed to allow the original owners to withdraw their own tokens.

This went down as a controversial decision in the history of Ethereum because the platform went against the behavior of blockchain technology which was mean to ensure that all transactions are irreversible.

Changing a blockchain repeatedly makes it more vulnerable and compromises its security. Hence, the hard fork violated the basic rules of the blockchain. However, a soft fork solution would be risky because failure would mean the destruction of Ethereum's public image.

So the Ethereum community split when taking the decision to go for a hard fork. The ones who did not give their consent today form the Ethereum classic and all the other members constitute Ethereum. Both these blockchains have the exact same features. Their only difference lies in how history played out.

Let's Start At The Very Beginning:

Blockchain was devised by someone who uses the pseudonym, Satoshi Nakamoto, to keep their identity secret.

This piece of technology is designed in such a manner that it allows the distribution of digital information without any additional requirement of copying.

The blockchain is changing the Internet as we know it because more and more industries are adopting it. While it was originally introduced for Bitcoin transactions, its other potential uses are slowly coming forward. Bitcoin is another type of cryptocurrency that has taken over the Internet in the last few years.

A blockchain is basically programmed in the form of a digital ledger which keeps a record of economic transactions. It may not be money that you want to track, but something else valuable and blockchain will allow you to do that.

There is one centralized database which is constantly updated with the addition of new data. You can imagine it as a spreadsheet that lists all new information in the same place so that you can access it easily.

A blockchain is a shared database where data is not stored in just one location which can be hacked into. Since the database is public and can be verified anytime, it is almost incorruptible. Millions of computer users can host a blockchain at the same time which makes it very convenient.

So What Is Ethereum?

Creating blockchain applications was never an easy task because it requires complex coding, cryptography and a comprehensive knowledge of mathematics. However, the tremendous leap in technology has opened a lot of doors. Applications which could not even be imaged before are now running and functioning well. Ethereum has made a niche for itself in this market by supplying developers with all the essential tools for creating decentralized applications.

Ethereum can be described as a decentralized platform which can efficiently run smart contracts on its very own custom built blockchain. The blockchain is extremely powerful and is a global infrastructure that can be adjusted when determining the value of any object or property.

Application developers will be able to create markets and keep a registry of all debts and promises. They will even have the power to transfer funds following specific instructions without having to go through a middleman. This will eliminate the risk that comes with involving a third party in any kind of transaction.

What Are Smart Contracts?

Smart contracts are actually a form of computer code which can help facilitate financial transactions and transfer of anything that has value including content, property, and shares. When these contracts are operating on the blockchain, they begin to act like self-built computer programmes. However, they only start working when all the required conditions are fulfilled.

These are applications which do not deviate from the original programming code when they are run. There is no possibility of downtime, fraud, third party interference or censorship disrupting the applications.

Mostly all blockchains can process code but there are certain limitations imposed on them. Ethereum transcends them and gives developers the ultimate power. It does not come with a list of operations but instead lets the developers create their own operations as and when they need it. Thousands of applications can be born from it which is what makes the platform so impressive.

Ethereum Virtual Machine:

Ethererum comes with the decentralized Ethereum Virtual Machine, commonly known as EVM. It has the task of executing scripts with the help of an elaborate international public network of nodes. Ether can be used as compensation for participant nodes after computations are done.

The EVM is essential for smart contracts to run properly because it provides the perfect environment. It is sandboxed and kept separately away from the network and the host computer system. All the nodes run an EVM implementation and work according to the instructions they receive.

Ethereum Virtual Machines are compatible with Go, Haskell, C++, Java, Ruby, Rust, JavaScript and Python.

The EVM is a Turing complete software which will let you run any programme you want on the network under the correct conditions.

It has simplified the process of creating blockchain applications and made it more efficient than it ever was before.

The platform also has a transaction pricing mechanism embedded internally which is called Gas. It eliminates spam and ensures proper allocation of resources.

Is Ethereum Different From Bitcoin?

Ethereum bears a similarity to Bitcoin in being a distributed public blockchain network. However, there are certain differences between the two that stand out.

The major difference between Ethereum and Bitcoin is that they were built for different purposes. As a result, they have distinct capabilities which they do not share with each other.

Bitcoin is actually just a part of the whole. It utilizes blockchain technology in one particular manner, that is to establish a peer to peer electronic cash system so that Bitcoin payments are successful. On the other hand, the Ethereum blockchain is helpful to create programming codes for decentralized applications. Ethereum does not let you mine for a digital currency. Instead, miners are supposed to work they can earn a crypto token called Ether which can enhance the network. Ether can be used as a tradeable cryptocurrency or as an asset to meet the monetary requirements for transactions and other services on the Ethereum network.

Why Does Ethereum Use Blockchain Technology?

Traditional servers are such that all your applications will have separate servers which will implement their code in isolated silos. This makes it difficult for the public to share data flexibly. The malfunctioning of even one application can end up affecting other users and software.

However, as a blockchain, users can create nodes which will have replications of the data that is necessary for both the nodes and the users. As a result, the user data remains strictly private while the applications are decentralized creating an easy space to work in.

What Can You Do With Ethereum?

If you are a developer who loves to experiment, then you will love the Etherum platform because it has so many different features to keep users fascinated. The flexibility of the design makes it a multi-faceted platform.

You can accomplish a lot by investing in Ethereum. Listed below are the most popular features of the platform.

Keep Your Assets Safe:

The Ethereum Wallet allows you to access all the decentralized applications which are available on the

Ethereum blockchain. The Wallet lets you hold and store the Ethereum currency, also known as Either along with any other crypto-assets that you build on Ethereum. You can be assured of the safety of your currency and valuables because the blockchain network allows little scope for malicious hacking. The Wallet can also be used if you are interested in deploying and using smart contracts. The easy template given with the Wallet will make creating contracts much easier.

Design A Cryptocurrency and Issue It For Use:

You know that the digital world has a large number of digital currencies now that can be used just as regular money to carry out different transactions. Do you want to create your very own tradeable digital token? You will be able to represent it as an asset which means that you will be able to use it as currency. It will also signify a virtual share and be a proof of membership. The tokens that you will create will have a standard coin API as a result of which your contract will be compatible with all wallets and other contracts automatically without you having to put in an extra effort.

You can fix the total amount of tokens which are to be in circulation or let it fluctuate. Now build your very own central bank which will issue your puzzle-based cryptocurrency for you.

Start your project with a crowdsale:

Lack of funds and resources is a huge obstacle for those who want to bring their ideas to fruition. If you are someone who has tons of ideas for Ethereum but needs help and funding to get the project going, then you can heave a sigh of relief. The platform itself has made provisions for such a situation. It allows you to create a contract that will keep the contributor's money till you reach a fixed goal. If you are successful, then you will receive the funding for the project. In case you fail to meet the deadline, then the money will be returned back. The best part about this system is that it does not require a centralized arbitrator which means that nobody has to depend only on trust. The crowdfund can help you pre-sell a product or even sell virtual shares on the blockchain platform.

Establish a democratic organization:

Once your idea has been implemented and the funds are in place, it is your duty to establish an organization that will be both democratic and autonomous. You can hire managers to look after everyday work. A loyal CFO will take care of all your accounts while you attend board meetings and engage yourself in paperwork.

However, Ethereum can make your work much easier. Once you draw a contract, it will gather enough proposals from all your supporters. Following that, it will submit them via a transparent voting process.

The external force in the form of a robot will run your organization to perfection. The main advantage of having a robot take decisions is that it will not give in to emotions or undue influence. It will only perform the tasks which are mentioned in its programme code. The decentralized Ethereum network will let you guarantee a 100% uptime on all your services. Based on shareholder voting, this association will surely be successful.

Create an absolutely new decentralized application:

For any developer, the most exciting part of a project is designing the main application and deciding how it will work. Ethereum is the perfect platform to develop your ideas because it is cryptographically secure and decentralized.

Projects on Ethereum:

The Ethereum platform gives birth to applications that span across a number of services and industries. which means that there is always a healthy variety. It is not possible to know which app will be successful till it is finished and put to the test, but there are new projects starting every day. Take a look at some of these interesting projects.

We fund is designed to make crowd-funding campaigns easier by providing an open platform where smart contracts can be made. The contributions are automatically changed into contractually backed digital assets which can then be used for transactions, both selling and trading.

BlockApps wants to help enterprises create, handle and deploy blockchain applications as easily as possible. It is integrated with the legacy systems and has full production systems. BlockApps has all the essential tools for creating private, semi-private and public blockchain applications for the different industries.

Provenance relied on Ethereum for help in making supply chains more transparent for consumers and the general public. It traced back the history of all products so that there is an open and accessible framework of information which people can consult before making purchases. Its main intention was to help the public make more informed choices.

With *Uport*, users can are in total control of information pertaining to their identity and personal life. It is a secure and convenient way to establish oneself as the sole decider of what can access what data about them. This application eliminates the need for third parties like government institutions as the user can change the visibility of their personal information any time they want.

Augur is a forecasting market platform and is one of the most interesting projects on Ethereum. If one can forecast an event correctly, then he or she is rewarded accordingly. This includes predictions about real-world events but the forecasting is done by the trading of virtual shares. A winning share leads to monetary benefit.

Conclusion:

While The DAO hack was an obstacle on the path of Ethereum's success, the platform is now moving on from it. Its user-friendly platform helps in harnessing blockchain technology like never before.

If you want to find more about Ethereum I recommend this book.

If decentralization was becoming popular earlier, then Ethereum has added an extra momentum to it. You can safely invest in Ethereum or start creating an app of your own.

Once upon a time, money was purely a physical asset. But times have changed, and today there are numerous digital currencies that are as effective as cash in handling transactions. Also called cryptocurrency, the digital currency has revolutionized the world of business as we know it.

After the Occupy Wall Street debacle, when major banks were accused of misusing their power and rigging the system, there arose a need for a transaction method that would not dupe clients into paying exorbitant fees.

Bitcoin was devised by Satoshi Nakamoto whose identity remains unknown till date. It is effective in eliminating the middleman and increasing the transparency of the process during transactions. To make sure that the system of Bitcoin worked to perfection, Satoshi conceptualized the first ever blockchain in the history of technology. The decentralized system or a blockchain allowed the user to be in charge of his or her funds all the time.

This cryptocurrency has gained immense global popularity in just a short while since it works without a central bank and is completely based on a peer-to-peer network. All transactions can be verified with the help of network nodes after which it is noted in the blockchain register that resembles a public distributed ledger. This ledger is constantly updated with information every minute.

The process is almost immune to hacking which means that your funds will always be secure. Since there is no single database that contains all the valuable data of the users, it is incorruptible.

Conclusion

Thank you again for downloading this book!

I hope this book was able to help you .

Finally, if you enjoyed this book, then I'd like to ask you for a favor, would you be kind enough to leave a review for this book on Amazon? It'd be greatly appreciated!

Click here to leave a review for this book on Amazon!